How to Simplify Your Life

Change Your Mind for Better Now and Happier Tomorrow

Anthony Glenn

Copyright © 2019 Anthony Glenn

All rights reserved.

ISBN: 9781092230216

Photography by Kristina Vorobeva

Contents

Introduction 5
1. Decide on your priorities. 9
2. Evaluate your engagements. 10
3. Evaluate your time. 12
4. Learn to say no 13
5. Limit your communication, information, media ... 14
6. Simplify your online life. 15
7. Purge and declutter everything before organizing. 18
8. Change your buying habits. 23
9. Free up time. 24
10. Then fill your time. 25
11. Do what you love. 26
12. Spend time with people you love 26
13. Spend time alone 26
14. Be present and aware. 27
15. Slow down. 28
16. Streamline your life - make simple systems. 31
17. Stop multitasking. 35
18. Create routines. 37
19. Learn what "enough" is. 41
20. Become a minimalist. 42
21. Quality before quantity. 43
22. Express yourself 43
23. Learn to relax. 44

24. Connect with nature. 46
25. Eat healthily. 46
26. Exercise. 47
27. Find inner simplicity. 48
28. Leave some space in your schedule. 49
29. Learn to do nothing. 49
30. Ask "Does this simplify my life? Does this make me happy?" 51

Introduction

"If you don't have fifteen minutes in a day for meditation, then meditate for thirty!"

Can you remember the last time you enjoyed the sunset? When was the last time you told a child, "yes, we have enough time for one more story,"? And then you read it slowly and consciously, or talked to them until they fell asleep, then watched them sleep for a while? When was the last time you had a lazy afternoon, a lazy coffee with a friend, without any rush or an urge to do something?

We aren't saying that you don't need to work, or that you don't have a lot of tasks to finish. We don't suggest you give up everything and move to a beach far, far away, to simply fish and swim all day every day for the rest of your life (although that's one amazing idea).
What we are saying is that if you don't have the time to stargaze, talk to a child, ask yourself how you are, to think, do nothing at all, something's wrong. Although that's a pretty common situation among people nowadays, that's not how things should be.

Why not?

Because you aren't actually living life – and it's passing you by. While you are focusing on your endless to-do lists, not having time to smell the roses, life is going on without you. It's your choice how you spend your time on this planet, but this is a very common trap most of us fall into. We are not aware that we have become a player in an endless game, a race exactly. We are all in a constant race, chasing more and more of everything - better achievements, more money, bigger houses, expensive things, and so on. What's the scariest part is the end of the game - there's no end. You can never catch that "enough." You can just fall down drained, only to be replaced by a new racer.

Is there an exit from the race?

Fortunately, yes. You can escape the game by becoming aware of it and then changing the rules for yourself. The only way to win the game is not to do what everybody else does - run faster, harder. You need to do the opposite - slow down. Leave the race, make your own rules, and change the goal.

That's all nice, but how can you find more time for that? We only have 24 hours in a day, and so many things to do that maybe even 30 hours wouldn't be enough.

The answer is in simplifying your life.

In this book, we will talk about the benefits that simplicity can bring you, and how to apply it to your life.

Why you should simplify your life

"Beauty is in simplicity," and, "Simplicity is the peak of civilization," do not refer only to art or culture. A general rule is that, "less is more," and that isn't about ladies make-up. Look around; you will find that the best things in the world are the simplest. Nature is simple, and we should all follow it. Life is also meant to be simple. There's nothing simpler and better than just being alive and being present. Could you imagine a better feeling than love? It's so simple to love.

However, people often put barriers in their own way. We often think that we constantly have to solve problems, while, actually, we are the ones making them. Our lives are far more complicated than they should be. That's the first, most fundamental reason why you should make things simpler.

Furthermore, simplifying your life will bring you many benefits. When there are fewer distractors, you become more focused, can concentrate better, and are more productive. It's easier to see your vision and keep a focus on your goals, to be organized, to make reasonable plans, and stick to them. In a nutshell, you see what you want better and understand how to get there. It's easier to practice what you need to become the version of yourself you desire.

When things become more straightforward, there's less need to rush, less hustle and bustle, so you'll become calmer, peaceful, and mindful. That makes you present, and you can experience your life more deeply. You can finally enjoy it. You can do more of the things you love or gather new experiences - you don't have to wait until you're older or retired. This way, your life will become richer, fuller, more colourful, joyful, and entertaining. You'll get back your cheerfulness and playfulness.

A simple life has different meaning to different people. In this book, we will talk about simplifying your life by eliminating all but the most important. When you exchange chaos for peace, you are free to do what truly means something to you. That means that you need to get rid of everything that doesn't bring you any value to make the space for the important things, both literally and figuratively. You'll need to re-examine everything, from your belongings to contacts to habits and routines. To make space for new memories to come, you need to declutter first. To create time for people you love, you need to say 'no' to those who just drain your energy.

Being unbusy and having time for meaningful conversations, for playing with your children, for reading good books, learning new skills, visiting new places, enjoying doing nothing - these are all powerful reasons to throw away what doesn't serve you anymore and free up space and time for what really matters.

However, simplifying life is not a simple process. It's a journey, not a destination. The basic thought is that you should identify what is really important to you and eliminate everything else. That's the simplest explanation of how to simplify life. But the work ahead of you is not insignificant. What you need to do to get results is to apply those principles to all areas of your life.

1. Decide on your priorities.

What's most important in your life? Choose the four or five most important things you can't imagine life without. Your family, a partner, your career, friends, art? That is what really matters to you and for which you need more time and energy. Maybe you would like to spend more time with your kids, enjoying their childhood, being more present, physically and emotionally, improve and grow as a parent. Maybe you would like to do more in building or improving your career. Some extra time for working on your important goals will be better spent in a few hours than hanging around on a social network, for example. Do you spend enough quality time with your partner? Do you have enough time for enjoying each other, talking and connecting? What about your parents, do you visit them often enough? Don't wait for some better time to hug people you love, to spend time with them, and tell them you love them. There won't be a better time than now. **"Now" is the only time you can do anything.** What else is important to you? Maybe a friendship that needs to be grown. Are you a friend you would like to have? Are you a good listener, or is your mind constantly bouncing and jumping from one task to another?

That's why you need to understand your priorities. Otherwise, it may happen (and it happens all the time) that you have a million tasks put together on an endless list, from kid's parties to groceries to a dentist to some other appointment. You can never check them all off, and you can never feel relaxed, calm, and entirely present.

2. Evaluate your engagements.

Look at everything that's going on in your life, from work to home to hobbies to kid's activities to different projects. Think about which of these you truly enjoy doing and which give you value. Are these activities in line with the 4-5 most important things you listed above? Drop those that aren't in line with your priorities.

List all the commitments in your life. Here are some typical ones:

Work - list the obligations you have at work. If you have a side job, you have even more responsibilities, so list them too.

Family – every role you play in the family (a husband, wife, parent, daughter, son) comes with more commitments — inventory yours.

Kids – each of the kid's commitments is yours, too. So, you may have soccer, basketball, choir, ballet and many more.

Home – we all have chores and home duties.

Hobbies – maybe you love running or cycling, painting or modeling, or something else; although each hobby you enjoy doing brings a lot of joy, it also comes with commitments.

Civic – if you volunteer or take part in some non-profit organization, that brings commitments, too.

Religious – you may attend church or go to service once a week.

Online – besides everything else, you may be active on a forum or mailing list or some online group. Being a part of an online community comes with commitments too.

You might have other categories. List everything.

Now, look closer at each thing from the list, and ask yourself: How important is this to me? Does this give me value? Is it in line with my values, goals, and life priorities? Could I drop it? Would it affect my life if it was gone?

These questions may be hard, but if you could eliminate just one of your commitments, that would be great for simplifying your life. See which of these things is not worth your effort and time, which one brings you the least in return. Maybe you have something on your list which is not in line with your priorities. Try to cut it out for a few weeks to see how you are without it. Then you can revisit your list and maybe cut something else. Keep only those activities that mean something to you and bring you value.

You may feel guilty every time you cut out some commitment because others will be disappointed. But it's a huge relief not having to do it each day, week or month when it's something you don't want to. Cutting it out will make space for something more important to you. It's crucial to have your priorities in mind, not what others expect from you.

If you take the time to edit your commitments, you'll thank yourself for a much more simplified life.

3. Evaluate your time.

Life is what's going on day by day, from the moment you wake up until you go to sleep. To simplify your life, you need to redesign your day. Monitor your activities. How do you spend your day? What do you do from the time you open your eyes until you fall asleep? Make a detailed list, and evaluate each individual thing, ask yourself if it is in line with your priorities. For every single activity during the day ask yourself: Does this make me happy? Does it bring my life some value? Does this get me closer to my goals? Do I enjoy doing it?

Then eliminate the things that don't fit you, keep only what's essential and sparks joy in you. Focus all of your attention and energy on those things.

4. Learn to say no.

If you can't say no, you won't have time to say yes to what you want. You will take on too much and spread yourself thin. That's the recipe for accomplishing nothing, at least to do nothing well. That's why saying no is one of the key habits you should learn if you want to simplify your life.

Why is it so hard?

We would rather sound positive and say yes to everything. We are taught it's polite and we don't want to offend people. But that way we often sacrifice our precious time for doing something more important.

One more reason is that we make obligations to people believing that our future self will want it and will be able to handle everything. But, that way, commitments pile up, and we have too many tasks to do.

If you want to simplify your life and finally have time and space for yourself, your priorities, and things you really like, you have to learn to say no.

How can I learn that?

By repeating. If you say it enough times, it will stop sounding so unpleasant. Also, people will get used to the possibility of being rejected by you.

Appreciate your time. Your time is limited, so don't waste it on things, people, and projects that are not in line with your values and priorities.

Be kind. Of course, you need to stay polite while rejecting people. But it's crucial to defend your time. You can say in advance that your schedule is full before the request is made.

You can complement the idea, person, or the project, but say it's not the right fit or the right time for you.

Don't apologize. "I'm sorry, but I don't have time," may be a polite, but it's a weak message. Don't be sorry for managing your time according to your priorities.

5. Limit your communication, information, media.

Limit your communication. Our lives these days are filled with an enormous flow of communication. So much so that it could consume your whole day if you let it. There are emails, cell phones, instant messages, Skype, Facebook, Twitter, Instagram, forums, paper mail, and more. If you don't want it to take up all your time, you need to limit your communication. It may be a good solution to only check email a certain number of minutes, at certain times of the day. Also limit the time spent on messaging, phone calls, social networking, and any other type of communication. Set a schedule for your communication and stick to it. It may be strange at first, but you will save a lot of time for more meaningful things.

Limit your media consumption. If media consumption is important to you, that's okay. But media in our life - the Internet, TV, radio, magazines - can dominate us. Be aware of that possibility and don't let it happen. When you limit media usage, that would affect your information consumption and simplifying your life. Like we said about limiting communication, try to limit media consumption too, schedule it for a specific time of the day.

One hidden enemy of the simple life is advertising. It's designed to make us want things, and it works. Reducing your consumption of advertising would also be smart. Think about the ways you are most exposed to advertising - it may be online, or in print, or elsewhere. Find ways to reduce it, and you'll be surprised how many fewer things you want.

6. Simplify your online life.

1. Keep your email inbox empty.
2. If your email inbox is full of new and read messages, it may make you feel overwhelmed. If the messages just keep piling up, it's normal.

But you would be more efficient and peaceful if you simplify your online life - email included.
3. Why is a full inbox stressful? It's because all of those emails telling us about the tasks we didn't take care of. It's like having a huge to-do list of unfinished obligations.

What's secret of inbox zero?

It's simple - check email regularly, and don't put it off for later. Take action on each email right away (or note it on a to-do list) and archive.

If you have tons of emails coming in and piling up, you can cut back the amount. You can unsubscribe from mailing lists, block people who always send you chain emails, automatically filter things that are coming to your inbox, avoid common questions by making "Frequently Asked Questions" on your website, and so on. Unsubscribe from all the newsletters that don't bring you value or pick just one source of news you read. This will all help.

Social networks

You can apply the same ideas to social networks as well. Reexamine what you watch, what you read, who you follow. For each group or post ask yourself, "Does this spark joy in me? Does this bring me value? Is this in line with my priorities and goals?" Then declutter your virtual social life. You can always unfollow, unlike, unfriend or block. Personalize your profiles in a way that you see only what's interesting, amusing, useful, or meaningful to you. If you realize that all the social network thing is not meaningful to you, you can take radical steps and leave it totally by deleting your profile. If this is too radical for you, there's nothing wrong with keeping it. The thing is - don't let it rule your life. And be careful about the time you spend on social networks because it may easily happen that you waste too much time watching what's going on in other people's lives instead of doing something meaningful with yours.

Schedule your time for being logged in. Your loved ones will be thankful.

Digitalized memories

There's no point in keeping photographs with no purpose. You wouldn't like to have a bad photo in your physical album. You also wouldn't want to look at a picture of something unpleasant which brings you bad memories. Likewise, you are not obligated to save them on your hard drive. Permit yourself to delete all poor-quality photos and those which are associated with something you don't like. Holding onto poor and unloved images makes it difficult to find good ones when you want to. Try to delete them before the import. And before that, eliminate those that are already there. The memories you keep, both physical or digital, should be those you love, and their point is to recall happy memories.

7. Purge and declutter everything before organizing.

You have probably noticed the difference between how you feel when you step into a messy room, with dust everywhere and all sorts of stuff lying around, and the feeling you have stepping into a tidy, neat place. There's nothing more relaxing than waking up in the morning and walking into a clean, decluttered room. Having an organized, neat house, brings peace and mental clarity.

On the other hand, when you step into a cluttered space, dirty, with stuff everywhere, your mind becomes restless, and stress levels rise.

So, if you want to simplify your life and improve your mindset, decluttering and tidying your space is an unavoidable step.

If you have never decluttered before, this will be a lot of work. If you already practice it, you know it's something that has to be done from time to time.

At the start, look around your space and think about your stuff. Do you have too many clothes you don't even wear? Are there piles of paper everywhere? Too many broken toys?

It's time to make space for good to flow in, for new memories, and new, better things you will love and use.

You can do decluttering and organizing room by room or go through different categories of stuff - whatever works for you. If you decide to work according to categories, choose one group and commit to decluttering and tidying it for a couple of days. You need to declutter clothing, kitchen and other home stuff, papers, books, and things with an emotional value. Pick all the things from one category and put them together. Then decide for every single item if you are going to keep it or toss it. Prepare boxes for donating and for throwing away. Take everything, even the tiniest thing from a pile and ask yourself if you are using it and love it. If not, but the thing is in good condition, donate it. If it's worn-out, torn, spoiled, broken - throw it away. If you love the item, use it, and want to keep it, then put it in its place. You should finish with fewer things, nicely arranged in their right places.

If you decide to declutter and tidy room by room, the main principle is the same. Here are some specifics about it:

It would be best to work one room per week until you have the whole house decluttered and tidy.

First, choose a room to focus on for a week. Don't try to do the whole house at once, because you may feel overwhelmed and lose motivation. Commit to the task for 15 minutes each day, unless you feel extra motivated to do more.

At first, skip things that are in closets, out of sight, and focus first on the things you can see.

Remove furniture you don't love or don't use. Also, remove big items like boxes full of stuff.

Clear all flat surfaces. Remove all little pieces of junk, knick-knacks, piles of paper or stuff, everything from tabletops and countertops, desktops, floors, and so on. Put it in a heap on the floor. Get two boxes and a trash bag and sort all the things from the pile, one by one. Decide for each item what you are going to do with it - throw it away, give it away, or put it in a place. Put back only select items on the flat surfaces - things that really belongs there, like a framed photo. Try to leave the flat surfaces as bare as possible. For all the stuff you removed, find its proper place - a drawer, a container, a shelf.

Repeat this process with the floors, removing everything that doesn't belong there. Then do the same with all the surfaces, like walls, refrigerator, stuff under tables, and so on. Leave only the things you need and love.

In the next phase, it's time to declutter your drawers, shelves, and closet. Although you can't see the clutter from there, every time you open the closet or drawer, you will see it again, and that affects your inner peace. So, it's time to move on to the drawers in creating simpler, stress-free spaces.

Empty everything from a drawer, clean it and toss all the junk from it.

Now go through the remaining stuff and sort it out: stuff you want to keep in the drawer, stuff that belongs elsewhere, stuff you'd like to give away. Try to keep related stuff in the drawer - only what belongs there - craft supplies, or underwear, for example.

Put the things back neatly, in an orderly manner. You should have a significantly reduced the amount of stuff to put back in the drawer.

Now, celebrate, and keep it that way! Never just toss stuff in the drawer. Make a habit of putting things where they belong and putting them back in a particular order.

When it comes to your closet, it's obvious why you need to keep it organized and clutter-free. It's pretty stressful when your clothes are overflowing, but you actually don't have anything to wear. Or you wear almost the same thing every day, but it's not easy to find those few things in all that clutter. So, here is some advice on decluttering your wardrobe:

Pull out all the clothes, and then decide for each item if it stays or goes.

Anything you haven't worn for a year should be donated.

If you like an item, but it doesn't fit, give it away. Don't keep things just because you want to lose weight and hope it will fit one day. You'll buy better pieces when you need them.

If an item is torn or stained, toss it away. If it is in good condition but doesn't match other things you own, or it's out of style, donate it.

When it comes to seasonal clothes, like swimsuits or a warm winter jacket, a good solution would be to store it in a separate closet, or a labeled container.

If you repeat this regularly, every few months, and refrain from buying too many unnecessary clothes, your closet will stay organized and be a relaxing cup of tea for your eyes and soul.

Everything we've said about decluttering drawers and closets, you can apply to each category or each room. Here are some more general pieces of advice:

Baby steps. To avoid overwhelming yourself and giving up on decluttering, set aside just fifteen minutes to tackle only one shelf or drawer. Then grab another task the next day.

If that seems too slow and doesn't work for you, set aside a few hours or more to declutter everything at once.

Take everything out. Then clean the drawer or shelf, and sort everything from a pile. Put only what you are keeping back and organize it.

Sort everything from a pile, making quick decisions.

Be merciless - if you didn't use it for a year, you will hardly use it again. Everything you don't use, you don't like, don't need, or don't have space for – toss it away, or give it to someone who can use it.

Go paperless. Keep only extremely important papers like birth, death and marriage certificates, insurance, warranties, wills, and other documents like that.

Create systems that work, make decluttering your new habit to prevent things accumulating.

Don't forget to celebrate when you are done. Enjoy the simplicity of your space and know that you have done something good to simplify your life.

8. Change your buying habits.

If you enjoy the neat and breathable look of your decluttered home, you won't want to pack it out again.

Besides that, while decluttering, you will become aware of how many useless things you have been buying and hoarding, and how much money and energy you spent on it. There are far better ways to spend money and time and much better uses for your space.

So, not only do you need to go through all your belongings from time to time, but you should also limit your buying habits.

To avoid compulsive shopping, try to plan all your buying in advance. Make a list of necessary items and stick to it.

It would be smart to limit your exposure to advertisements and avoid shopping malls. It's better to buy exactly what you need in smaller stores.

If you truly wish to buy something, give it some time. Write your wish down and wait for thirty days. If you still want it after that period, then buy it.

Consider buying used instead of new. This is an eco-friendly approach, and besides that, it will save you a lot of money. Moreover, while searching for it in a second-hand store, flea markets and so on, you won't be exposed to more advertisements.

9. Free up time.

You may feel like you have limitless time. But the truth is, our time on this planet is limited, and we often take it for granted until it's too late and we can't go back. It may sound scary, but the number one regret of the dying is that they didn't do enough of what they loved, they wasted time on other things. Don't let yourself feel the same; learn from other's experiences. Find ways to free up time for what really matters to you. That means eliminating all the things that don't nourish your soul or enrich your life. This refers to everything (both physical and non-physical) you don't like and enjoy. To make room for what you want to do, you need to cut back on time wasters. To make enough time to do more of what you love, you have to say no to something you don't like. For example, refuse to go to one more party to afford yourself some time for reading. In the same way, if you want to spend some time with your loved ones, you need to say no to another casual coffee with people whose company you don't enjoy too much. All of these "sacrifices" will pay off multiple times in your happiness and the sense of inner peace.

10. Then fill your time.

Why do that again when I've been doing so much to free it up?

Simplifying isn't meant to leave your life empty – its purpose is to make space in your life for what you really want to do. You need to know what those things are before you start simplifying.

If you decide what's most important to you and then get rid of the stuff that's not related to your priorities, what do you have left? Just the essential stuff you really care about and love to do. When you get rid of the other stuff, when you cut, for example, watching tv shows and series or hanging out on social networks from your life, don't just cut it out – replace it with what's important to you and what you love to do. That may mean that you will spend more time with your family instead of working, go surfing or running, reading or writing instead of watching TV.

The purpose of freeing up your time is not in doing nothing. It's in having more time for doing what you want. Be wise and don't let your work encroach on your new free time. Or don't waste it doing other things you don't enjoy so much. Use your renewed schedule wisely and purposely, for nourishing your soul - spending it with your loved ones, taking a walk or practicing a hobby, practicing self-development and mindfulness, playing sport, anything that makes you feel truly happy.

11. Do what you love.

Once you have some extra free time, be sure to spend it exclusively doing things you love. Look again at your list of 4-5 essential things. Do those, and nothing else.

12. Spend time with people you love.

Again, your list of essential things probably contains some of the people you love. If you somehow forgot to put them among your priorities, you may want to re-examine your list. Whether those people are your children, a partner, a spouse, parents, other family members, friends, or whoever, find time for them. Spend some quality time together regularly - do fun things with them, talk, be intimate (not necessarily in a sexual way), grow your relationship. Remember that we all have limited time here and you need to use it to show them how much you care for them.

13. Spend time alone.

Although some people aren't comfortable with it, solitude is good for everyone. It demands practice to get used to the silence and get in touch with your inner voice. It may sound new age, but it's incredibly calming. This quiet is healing and necessary for finding what's important to you.

When you make space for me-time, you can use it in different beneficial ways. Working on your self-development is one of the most precious investments you can do for your well-being.

Use your alone time for meditation, introspection, writing, gratitude, prayer, reflection, or other wonderful techniques to bring peace and success to all areas of your life.

More ideas and advice about how to practice mindfulness and self-growth techniques can be found in my book "Mental Hygiene: How to Change Your Mind".

14. Be present and aware.

This concept is so simple that it will spread its simplicity to other areas of your life, too. Living in the moment, present here and now, keeps you aware of everything that's going on around you and within you. It does wonders for your inner peace and efficiency.

Keep your focus on the here and now. Our thoughts constantly bring us to the past or the future. Don't follow them; stay in the present. Just notice your thoughts as they are coming and let them go. It helps if you focus on the sensations in your body, purposely concentrating on each part by part.

You may also put focus on the senses - touch, smell, sight, taste. Notice and feel as much as you can in the moment.

That's the way kids and animals experience life, and it's so relieving. In fact, that's the way things should go. We are not meant to be our thoughts, to think all the time, and follow each thought that pops up in our mind. We are the masters of our minds. You are the one who should decide whether to think or not about something. You are the one who chooses to stay consciously in this moment or to leave it. This way, you will feel incredibly calm, but also experience much more of your life, because the present is the only reality we have. Everything else is just an illusion.

15. Slow down.

Too often we run too fast through our lives and hardly catch a moment to simply enjoy. That's a real shame considering how much we are missing out on by being in a constant rush. We are pretty much like a hamster running on a wheel - there's often no point in our running. Life should be more about a journey, not a destination. In the end, where are you hurrying to? To the final end? Wouldn't it be smarter to enjoy the journey instead? Things are much simpler when you slow down. You won't accomplish as much as when you are doing everything fast, but what is the point of living life going from one task to another? Only to check them off and repeat them another day? If you focus on quality instead of quantity, it will become less chasing, and more enjoyable. Give yourself enough time to do everything with a whole heart and full attention. Don't just switch from one to another. Whatever you are doing during the day, give yourself time to be present, to notice and feel. Low the tempo and give yourself some free time for thinking or daydreaming, observing the world around you, or simply do nothing, being unbusy. Yes, we are all taught that it's wasting time, and it's almost forbidden to do nothing, it's considered lazy. But who says it's right? The truth is, life is more about how we feel, not about what we are doing.

Slowing down is not about doing less. It's not that you need to be lazy and non-productive. On the contrary, it's about putting quality before quantity, doing everything with your full attention, and with less stress. It's wise not to be a hamster on a wheel in a time of globalization, and constant rush and craziness.

Try to be mindful whatever you are doing. Be aware of everything that's going on in the moment inside you and around you, aware of your body, its movement, sensations, your thoughts, emotions, everything. Be fully present in that moment, don't rush mentally nor physically to the next step, next task, next day. When you feel the urge to hurry, to take fast action, to rush - just stop for a moment. Breathe. Slow down. Quiet your mind. Take leadership over your thoughts. Step out from the wheel. Smell the roses, and then, with all that fresh energy, you will accomplish more than you could in a hurry. The only thing you can get from constant rush is stress. And more stress. Also, it's the only thing you will lose if you slow down.

Eat slowly.

If you just swallow your food, you are not eating healthy, but you are also missing out on its great taste. If you slow down, it will bring you many benefits - weight loss, better digestion, and more joy. We all know that we should build healthy eating habits. But if you especially enjoy sinful foods, it's even more apparent how pointless it is just to swallow them. You are eating for joy, right? When you just gulp it, you have no time to enjoy it. It would be a much better solution to eat a small amount of it, but much slower. That way, you will enjoy much more in its taste, which is the only reason for eating bad food, and you will take in fewer calories too.

Even with healthy foods, drinks, or water, slowing down will improve your digestion, help you to lose weight, and bring you more happiness - in food and life generally.

When was the last time you enjoyed a glass of water? There are few feelings better than water in your mouth when you are really thirsty. When you slow down and start doing everything consciously, something as simple as drinking water becomes a pleasure.

Drive slowly.

Most of us rush through traffic every day, angry, frustrated, and stressed out. While doing so, we are endangering ourselves and others. Driving slower is safer, better on your fuel bill, and can be incredibly peaceful. Let some calm music play and enjoy the landscape. Use that time for contemplation, or brainstorming. And, of course, go to the right - you don't need to pay attention and get frustrated because you are annoying other drivers, but it's nice to be kind.

16. Streamline your life - make simple systems.

Many times, we have the feeling that our lives are chaotic and unstructured. That's because we use unplanned, complex systems we haven't given enough thought to.

A system is a certain way we handle things in our lives that happen regularly, like kids, lunches, email, laundry, etc. Any of these systems can be complicated or simple if you give it some thought. Start to simplify them, focusing on one system at a time (your paperwork, laundry, online life, tasks, etc.) The goal is to make them all simplified, efficient, and written. Then stick to it.

Here are some examples of systems, complicated and simple ones, just to give you a picture of what we're talking about. You will surely have your own list of systems, and probably a lot of ideas on what you should simplify.

Task systems

Complicated:

You go and pay one of your bills. But you forget to pay a second bill, so the next day you are running to do that during your lunch break. You need some food, so you go to the grocery store. When you get home, you realize that you forgot the milk, so you have to go again. The next day after work, you go to the store and pick up some dog food. But you forgot that you are having a party next weekend, so the next day you drive all over town getting things ready for it. Lots of wasted time, gas, and driving.

Simple:

You plan a particular day for grocery and errands. You prepare an errands list and a grocery list. Before this day, plan your menu for the next two weeks and complete your grocery list. Then plan your route for the next day, and the order of errands to finish. On the day you reserved for these tasks, you spend a couple of hours doing all the chores on your list and then buying all your groceries. This will save you a lot of effort, multiple shopping trips, gas, and time.

Laundry System

Complicated:

When you take your clothes off, you usually leave them on a chair, where there's a pile building up. From time to time, you pick them up and move them to a basket or a pile in the laundry room. When you have time, you might throw them in a load, dry them, and then toss the clean clothes in another basket, on a chair or on your bed, where they sit until you need to wear them. Then you find out the clothes have become wrinkled in the meanwhile.

Simple:

Every time you take your clothes off, hang them if they're clean or put them in a basket. It's great if you have separate baskets according to color - one for whites, one for dark colors, etc. When one of them gets full, you throw it in the washer, dry them, fold them or hang them, and put them away. You could even designate a laundry day and have nothing to do with laundry for the rest of the week.

E-mail System

A complicated and chaotic email system is a recipe for disaster. First, if your email notifier is turned on all the time, this will distract you from anything you do during the day. When an email comes in, you stop whatever you are doing to check it. But, if you don't have time to reply or to take the action requested, you put it away for later. Your inbox is full all day long, and at the end of the day, you have an inbox overflowing, and too many tasks waiting. You don't know where to start..

What about this: You designate specific times for dealing with emails during the day (it may be an hour in the morning and an hour in the evening or 30 minutes three times a day or whatever works for you). The rest of the day, you turn off your email notification, so that you're not disturbed. When it's your email-time, you tackle them one at a time, from top to bottom, and immediately decide what you're going to do with them. You can either reply right away, put a task on a to-do list, forward, archive or delete an email. None of them stay in your inbox. At the end of processing emails, you've got all your tasks sorted and listed on a to-do list, all the emails answered, and zero-inbox, ta-da!

Think about your systems and put some effort into simplifying them. Your life will be simple and nicer.

Keeping your house clean and tidy also demands a system. If you don't want to spend a whole Saturday each week on cleaning, and still have a messy home, it would be smart to clean as you go. What does that mean? That means that you do quick cleanups during the day and week. Develop the habit of putting things in their place right after using them instead of leaving them to be cleaned later. Keep all the surfaces clean, with no additional stuff. Do quick pickups before going to bed or leaving the house. Make your bed each morning. Clean the bathroom (a tub, toilet, or sink) after each use. Hang your clothes after taking them off. All of these things demand only a few minutes but have a huge impact on the look of your home, and your inner peace. All these habits need some time and practice to be developed, but patience will pay off in multiple ways, in a tidy home and more free time for doing the things you love.

What could you simplify? Here are some examples of the common systems in our everyday life: Bills, mail, chores, kid's activities, school work, contacts and phone numbers, information from the web, and much more. Think about the areas that need improvement to work smoothly.

Give your systems names, write them down and hang them in a visible place. Stick to them and reevaluate them from time to time - step back and examine if your systems still work for you or if it is time to change something.

17. Stop multitasking.

Although it may seem like multitasking will help you accomplish more, it is actually less efficient, less productive, more complicated, stressful and makes you prone to mistakes.

Juggling everything at once won't lead you to better achievements; it will only drive you crazy until the whole system falls apart.

How can you do single-tasking in the era of informational and demand overload?

Here are some tricks.

1. Make a to-do list. Note down all the tasks waiting for you and list them by priority - most important first. Check them done as you finish.

   Make a list of the most important tasks each day. Decide on just three very important things you want to accomplish and set them as goals for the day. Instead of a long list of things you won't manage to finish, try with this simple three-item list. This will make you feel like you've accomplished a lot.
2. Have a paper or a notebook for instant notes and reminders.
3. Gather together all the coming stuff - create a physical inbox besides an email inbox.
4. Plan your day in advance. Leave some free space between tasks.
5. Eat the frog. Do the most important task first in the morning. If you finish two or three of your important tasks, you'll feel relaxed for the rest of the day.
6. Ignore everything else or turn off distractions if possible. While you are concentrating on an important task, turn off all notifications, don't answer the phone, and don't think about anything but the task. That way you'll increase productivity and accomplish more, so you won't need multitasking.
7. If you feel the urge to jump onto the next task, slow down, stop yourself and focus on the here and now. Breathe. Then bring your

focus back onto what's the most important task at the moment.
8. If the interruption is really urgent and can't wait for you to finish the task, put it off, but make a note on where you are, so you can move on when you get back to the task.
9. Take regular breaks and appreciate your unstructured time. Move, breathe, and enjoy life.

18. Create routines.

Why is it important to have routines?

Our life is made up of things we repeatedly do. If you do something every day, that affects your life overall. There is a compound effect, which says that small amounts of anything accumulate and can have a huge final impact. For example, if you are learning a new language for only 15 minutes each day, in a year or two you'll be able to speak that language. The same is for everything else. Only one extra cookie a day can make you fat in a few years. This one may be radical, but you get the idea of what we are talking about.

So, if you develop a habit of exercising, only for a half an hour a day, this will greatly affect your health. That's why our routines are essential. Besides that, having established routines makea you relaxed because you know what you can expect, and don't have to think about which steps you need to take next. For example, if you know you are always eating eggs for breakfast, you won't have to think about what to buy and prepare.

Our morning and evening routines are particularly important because they shape our life and what we are taking with us into a dream, and what we pick up first in the morning.

You need a morning routine that will help you wake up, energize yourself, and prepare for the day. It's up to you to create the rituals that work best for you and make them a habit. But here are some proven techniques and suggestions on what you could include in your morning routine:

- *Wake up early*

You don't have to get up extremely early like 4 a.m. (although many people do and say it's awesome). It's enough to wake up an hour earlier than you're used to, and you'll have extra time for yourself. This time in peace and solitude is the best way to set your energy for the day.

- *Hydrating*

Drinking enough water is vital for the whole day, but it should also be the first thing you do in the morning. Treat your body with a glass or two of fresh water to wake up the metabolism. Warm water with a few drops of lemon juice can make miracles for your health.

- *Exercising*

An easy workout, stretching and warm up is a wonderful way to kick start the day. If you prefer more dynamic exercises then you can run in the morning, cycle, or go swimming. If you are a fan of yoga, it's also the perfect time for a few asanas and greeting the Sun.

- Showering

Not only will you begin the day fresh, but you can also enjoy aromatherapy or under-shower meditation. Merely put your focus together with water onto each part of the body. Do your best to be mindful in these moments and feel intensively every drop on your skin.

- Working towards your goals

Doing something small, like 10-15 minutes, towards your big goals each day will take you a long way.

- Making plans

Morning is the perfect time for making plans for the day, creating your to-do and most-important-tasks lists.

- A healthy breakfast

Don't skip the most important meal of the day. Try to prepare a balanced breakfast, healthy, highly-nutritious, and delicious.

- Meditation

Use these moments for yourself, to connect with your inner being, and start the day peaceful, calm, and aware. Morning meditation will help you set the perfect vibration and mood for the coming day

- Reading

If you can't find time for reading, here it is. Choose something affirmative, wise, positive, and motivational to read. It's food for the soul. Breakfast for the soul - to be precise.

- *Writing*

When we wake up in the morning, our mind is calm, and our thinking is clear. It's the perfect time for writing your affirmations, book of gratitude, journal, morning pages, or whatever you like.

- *Gratitude*

Before anything else, begin each day with a sense of appreciation for all the blessings you have. After all, you woke up again, and that's enough of a reason to be grateful.

Your evening routine is also important - it will set you up for a fresh start the next day. Basically, what you should do in the evening is to calm down, review your day, plan the next one, clean the house, and prepare everything you will need in the morning.

Everybody's evening routine will be different, but here are some ideas on what can you do right before going to bed:
- go to sleep early
- set your alarm
- pack lunch for tomorrow
- do a quick cleanup and pickup
- prepare your clothes for the next day
- make a to-do list
- meditation and gratitude
- take a bath
- listen to calm music
- drink tea
- read to sleep

19. Learn what "enough" is.

We live in a materialistic society that encourages us to want more and more, with no end in sight. You will always want more of everything - more money, stuff, achievements, the latest gadget, a new car, new shoes, and clothes. It's nice to wish for something, but have you ever wondered when you will have enough? Most people don't know. They just run - chasing more and more, better and better, buying and accumulating, running from one wish to another without enjoying their accomplishments, or life, or anything at all. It's an endless cycle. What you need to do to escape is to figure out the meaning of the word "enough." What's enough for you? How much do you need or want to have? What are enough accomplishments? When is it enough work, or chasing something? And then stop when you get there. Repeat to yourself "it's enough" until you truly understand it. Enjoy your "enough." Be thankful for what you have instead of burning yourself out for more and more.

Also, decide what is enough when it's about demands from yourself. Do you have to be perfect to be satisfied? Do you need everyone to approve and appreciate you? Stop with that torture. You are enough. Simple as that. You are pretty, smart, tall, fit, whatever you are forcing yourself to be.

It may sound contradictory in a book about a self-development technique like this one, but you also need to decide when it's enough self-improvement. Don't be hard on yourself and force yourself to change. Be kind and loving instead. Have compassion and understanding and give yourself time, whether you are trying to develop a new habit, to lose weight, or to improve something else in your life.

20. Become a minimalist.

This one is so close to simplifying life, that it's almost the same thing. If not, it is certainly the basic principle that enables you to simplify. Becoming a minimalist means that you decide on what's most important to you and then you eliminate everything else. When you apply this approach to all areas of your life, the result is pure, simple life. So, that's not something applicable only to your belongings. That's just the most obvious level - you need to declutter and purge your possessions. Keep only those that bring you joy, and toss everything else.

But, you can declutter everything - from your desktop and wardrobe to your thoughts and emotions, your beliefs, relationships, contacts, hobbies, to duties, everything. Always keep only what you use and love and eliminate the rest. Be merciless.

Apply this concept to your mindset. Use meditation and contemplation to dig up all of your old beliefs that need to be reexamined. Which of them still serve you and which do you need to get rid of and replace with new ones? More about introspection and changing beliefs can be found in my book "The Law of Attractions: Your Guide to Satisfaction and Success".

Yes, that's also minimalism in action when you decide to do only one thing instead of multitasking. The same principle you use when you only keep the photos that recall happy memories and toss the rest away, or when you cut off all the coffees with random people to spend time only with those you love the most.

Yes, this one is crucial because it's the most important way to simplify.

21. Quality before quantity.

This one goes hand in hand with the one above. They are like salt and pepper - actually this is one of the basic principles of minimalism. Always choose to do less, buy less, talk less, anything less, if that means you will make better use of it. It's a better option to buy only one pair of jeans if it's one you'll wear for a long time rather than having three pairs of poor quality. The same goes with everything - choose to have some quality time with a loved one, instead of drinking coffees and have superficial chats with people you don't honestly care about.

22. Express yourself.

Finding a creative outlet for self-expression is a great way to replace much of the unnecessary work you've eliminated from your life. That's something extremely important for keeping your soul satisfied and cheerful. Yet too many of us underestimate the power of creativity and leave too little or no space at all for it. But the truth is that our soul needs to be fed just like our body. We usually don't consider a lack of self-expression as a cause of our anxiety or other poor feelings. It's time to change that. Be aware that your soul needs your attention. Your personality has to be expressed. You need some play and fun, and your talents are dying to be discovered - whether your passion is writing, playing music, painting, drawing, dance, creating movies, designing websites, skateboarding, whatever. Finding a way for self-expression brings joy and makes your life much more fulfilling. That's one of the things worth simplifying.

23. Learn to relax.

There will always be some stress in your life no matter how much you simplify it. So, you need to find ways to decompress after stress.

Here are some proven ways to do that:

- Deep breathing. Breathe slowly, take a deep breath, hold it for a moment, and then slowly let it out. Try to count to ten as you are exhaling. Let all the tension and stress leave your body with your breath. Repeat this until you feel your stress level has dropped.
- Take a walk to refocus. Physical activity and sensations from the outdoors will relax you.

- Exercise. No matter what kind of physical activity you choose, everything is good to melt your stress and give you some quiet time.
- Go outdoors. Even if you don't feel like exercising, just being outside, enjoying fresh air and sunlight will help you cut stress out of your system.
- Self-massage - Tense up and then relax each part of your body. You can apply self-massage to your shoulders, neck, head, and lower back.
- Having sex – No explanation required.
- Take a day-off - If it's possible for you, take a free day to center and calm. Allow yourself to take some time for yourself.
- Read - Getting lost in an imaginary world will take away all the stress of everyday life. Throw yourself down on the couch with an exciting book and disconnect from reality for some time.
- Disconnect - When it's about disconnecting, it's also a good idea - turn off the phone, the computer, and the outside world for a while.
- Meditation - You don't need any special knowledge or practice - just sit down in a quiet place and focus on your breathing, with closed eyes. Ignore all the thoughts that pop up. Just breathe for as long as you can. That's all.

- Take a nap – This is the best meditation and re-start button. So, press it from time to time.

24. Connect with nature.

In modern civilization, we have lost our connection with nature. Reconnect, and you'll find more fulfillment and pleasure. Use every opportunity to go outside, enjoy sun, grass, sea, sand, or rain, snow - the point is to be in the fresh air and to feel alive.

Nature is extremely simple and beautiful in its simplicity. We should all learn from it. We are the ones who make things complicated. Nature is always absolutely simple and perfect.

25. Eat healthily.

Maybe it's not obvious how eating healthily is related to simplicity, but, believe me, it is. If you eat unhealthily - fatty, salty, sugary foods all the time, it's only a matter of time until you develop medical issues. And life with an illness is not a simple one; it includes frequent doctor visits, taking medications, therapy, and so on. Eating healthy simplifies all of that and pays off in the long term.

You don't have to choose between complicated meals and eating fast food. There are numerous ways to prepare healthy, yet simple, meals. But you need to put some thought into it.

You don't want to spend the whole life by the stove. And don't want to use a million ingredients. Make it as simple as you possibly can.

We don't need the mountain of calories that fast food offers. This will only make you fat, which is stressful and brings complications, and also lacks real nutrients. What we need are vitamins, minerals, protein, good fats, fiber, etc.

When you apply all of the simplifying systems to your diet, you'll eliminate a lot - processed food, fast food, fried, sugar, maybe dairy, soda, and so on. You'll be left with only the essentials. That will enable you to make simple and quick, yet tasty meals, without wasting time.

You should also simplify the amount of food you eat. What's the simplest amount? It's one portion, not too little or too big, just enough to stop your hunger. So, eat only when you are hungry. You don't need to starve yourself, but you also don't need to stuff yourself with healthy food. So, no huge portions, no second or third serving. Stick to a normal portion. Be creative, give it a thought and do some research. Then you can plan your menu for two weeks. It's important to have three main meals, snacks and treats from time to time. Include fresh fruits, veggies, white meat, fish, nuts, and you can make delicious miracles.

26. Exercise.

This one goes hand in hand with a healthy diet. But exercising goes a bit further - it will also help you stay healthy in the long run, and helps to remove stress and improve mood.

However, the hardest part is that, if you are not used to working out, you need to put some effort into building the habit. That's why many people don't do it. However, although it may be simpler not to begin at all, it's far simpler to stay healthy, in good shape, and vital in the long run.

So, don't hesitate to put effort into it. Move your butt and start moving. You can walk, run, dance, swim, go to the gym, cycle, whatever makes you happy as long as it makes you sweat.

Start slow and easily, taking baby steps, and then strengthen your training as your abilities improve.

27. Find inner simplicity.

You don't have to be a spiritual person to see how spending some time with your inner-being turns chaos into peace and simplicity. It can be done through meditation, other self-development techniques, or through prayer and communicating with God. Find out more about the ways to reconnect with your inner-self in my book "How to Heal Your Soul: Your Path to Peace of Mind".

28. Leave some space in your schedule.

Try to put some free time between your obligations and tasks. Why? To be unbusy, to do what you want, or simply to do nothing.

29. Learn to do nothing.

Do you know how to do nothing?

Sure, we all know how to waste time. But that's not what we are talking about here. There is a huge difference between laying around and losing time while your mind is skipping from one thing to another, surfing the Internet or changing channels on TV, against truly relaxing and enjoying nothingness. And that's something many of us don't know how to do. When you know how to do it right, that will decompress you from stress and make you efficient when you actually work.

As with every other technique, doing nothing demands some practice. So, start small at first. Go to a quiet place, turn off all the distractors. Sit or lay down, close your eyes and enjoy doing nothing for a little as ten minutes at the beginning. Practice this every day, as much as you can.

Focus on your breathing, like in meditation. If you keep your focus on breathing in and out, that will lower the chances of other thoughts distracting you. When they come, you already know - ignore them, and focus again. We are not here to think; we are learning to do nothing.

The next step in doing nothing is relaxing. If you don't know how to do that, look at cats and dogs, they are masters at it. Find a comfortable space without distractors and lay down. You can take a nap, that means that you are already relaxed enough. If not, you can apply self-massage, or tense and relax each part of the body. Combine it with breathing techniques and enjoy the feeling.

One more fantastic way of doing nothing is to do nothing in a warm bath, with bubbles and different scents (even if you are a male). Of course, turn off all the distractions and notifications. Tell everyone not to disturb you, even if there's an emergency.

You can focus on the taste and smell of beverages or food. Enjoy a cup of coffee, or tea, or some food like soup, fruit, or a dessert. Focus on the liquid or every bite, sipping it or chewing slowly, to savor its taste. Feel the flavor and the texture. You can even close your eyes to enjoy it completely. This goes very well with doing nothing.

You can go outside and try to do nothing in nature. It doesn't have to be somewhere far or wild. It's enough to go to your backyard, or a park, a wood, near a lake, or a beach. Sit still and focus on the sensations around you - the landscape, plants, wildlife, water. Appreciate nature and enjoy the silence. Don't let the mind wander, focus on here and now.

When you master doing nothing, it's time to incorporate this into your daily life. For example, you can do it while you are waiting for something. While you are waiting in a line, on a bus, a plane, or an office. Don't try to use this time writing your to-do list. Don't look at your phone. Don't worry about what you have to do next. Just be present, wait, and do nothing else. Try some relaxation techniques, like breathing. Watch the people around you.

You can also try to do nothing while you are driving. Do nothing besides driving - don't talk on the phone, don't eat, don't listen to music. Just focus on driving, the road, and your breath. And be careful not to crash, of course.

Finally, when you become a master of doing nothing, you'll be able to do it in the middle of chaos. When it's a stressful day at work or with the kids, just shut out everything around you and focus on your breathing. This will make you calm and productive with any task in hand.

It may sound absurd, but doing nothing is not easy, and it demands regular practice. Begin today!

30. Ask "Does this simplify my life? Does this make me happy?"

Always ask yourself these questions while considering something - whether it's an activity, people, stuff. Ask for the things you already have in your life, and for the new ones when they come.

If the answer is yes, keep it, or go ahead.

If the answer is no, reconsider it. You don't want anything which brings you in the opposite direction of your goals.

Now you have thirty more ideas on how you can simplify your life. That will bring you more peace and fulfillment than you could ever imagine.

You don't have to apply all of them to experience the difference. Choose those you like the most and try to incorporate them into your daily life. When you feel the difference, you will probably want to try out more of them.

Life is a precious gift. You've got an opportunity to make your heaven on Earth. Use simplicity to achieve that.